Destination Detectives

China

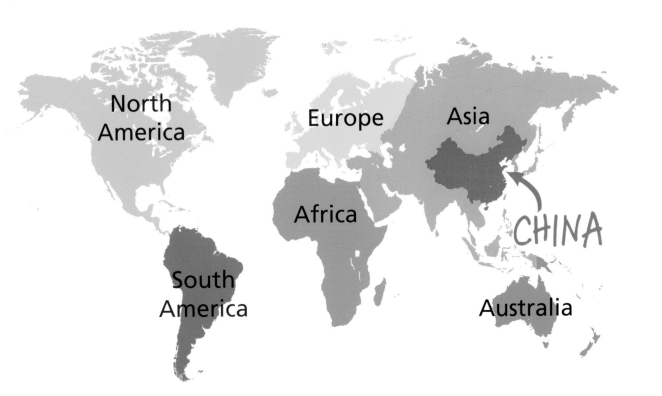

North America

Europe

Asia

CHINA

Africa

South America

Australia

Ali Brownlie Bojang

Chicago, Illinois

Produced for Raintree Publishers by Discovery Books Ltd
Printed in Hong Kong

11 10 09 08 07
10 9 8 7 6 5 4 3 2 1

Library of Congress Cataloging-in-Publication Data
Brownlie Bojang, Ali, 1949-
   China / Ali Brownlie.
      p. cm. -- (Destination detectives)
   Includes bibliographical references and index.
   ISBN-13: 978-1-4109-2929-7 (lib. bdg.)
   ISBN-10: 1-4109-2929-9 (lib. bdg.)
   ISBN-13: 978-1-4109-2940-2 (pbk.)
   ISBN-10: 1-4109-2940-X (pbk.)
   1. China--Juvenile literature. 2. China--Geography--
Juvenile literature. I. Title. II. Series.
   DS706.B735 2007
   951--dc22

                                          2005032916

This leveled text is a version of *Freestyle:
Destination Detectives: China*. Produced for Raintree by
White-Thomson Publishing Ltd.

Acknowledgments
The Art Archive pp. 17 (William Sewell); Corbis pp.
9 (Reuters), 10 (Keren Su), 13 (Xinhua), 15t (Royal Ontario
Museum), 28 (Ron Watts), 29 (Keren Su), 33 (Chi Haifeng/
Xinhua), 38 (Michael S. Yamashita), 38–39 (Vince Streano);
Photolibrary pp. 4–5 (Pacific Stock), 7 (IFA-Bilderteam
Gmbh), 10–11 (Panorama Stock Photo), 12 (Panorama
Stock Photo), 15b (Pacific Stock), 19 (Index Stock Imagery),
20–21 (Panorama Stock Photo), 21 (Panorama Stock Photo),
24 (Panorama Stock Photo), 27 (Panorama Stock Photo), 31
(Panorama Stock Photo), 34 (Botanica), 35 (Pacific Stock),
37, 40 (Daniel Cox), 41 (IFA-Bilderteam Gmbh), 42
(Panorama Stock Photo); TopFoto pp. 16 (Nathan Strange/
uppa.co.uk), 25 (Image Works); WTPix pp. 5t, 5m, 5b, 6, 8,
14, 18, 22, 23l, 26t, 26b, 30, 32, 36, 43.

Cover photograph of lion dance reproduced with permission
of Panorama Stock Photo Co., Ltd/OSF/Photolibrary.

Thanks to Luo Jailing and Simon Scoones.

Every effort has been made to contact copyright
holders of any material reproduced in this book.
Any omissions will be rectified in subsequent
printings if notice is given to the publishers.

The paper used to print this book comes from
sustainable resources.

Disclaimer
All the Internet addresses (URLs) given in this book were valid
at the time of going to press. However, due to the dynamic
nature of the Internet, some addresses may have changed or
ceased to exist since publication. While the author and
publishers regret any inconvenience this may cause readers, no
responsibility for any such changes can be accepted by either the
author or the publishers.

Contents

Any words appearing in the text in bold, **like this,** are explained in the glossary. You can also look out for them in the Word Bank box at the bottom of each page.

Where in the World?

You wake with a start. There's a lot of noise outside. You look out of the hotel window. You can see children laughing and shouting. They are watching firecrackers going off.

It's almost midnight. People start to count down: "Three, two, one! *Xin nian yu kuai!* Happy New Year!" Fireworks light up the sky.

► Lion dances are performed at New Year celebrations. Chinese people believe lions bring good luck.

It is the Chinese New Year. These celebrations start sometime between January 30 and February 20. They start when there is a new moon. They end fifteen days later.

This is a noisy and colorful introduction to China. You are in the city of Beijing. Beijing is the capital of China. Your journey starts here.

Find out later...

...where you can see the world's largest palace.

...why this huge wall was built.

...what this type of exercise is called.

So This Is China!

You notice a map of China on the wall. It is a huge country. It is only slightly smaller than the United States. Some other traveler has stuck notes on the map.

Strangely shaped hills are found in the southern regions of Yunnan and Guizhou. They are made of a type of rock known as **limestone**.

The Chang Jiang River is 3,987 miles (6,380 kilometers) long. It is the third-longest river in the world. It runs from the mountains in the west to the East China Sea.

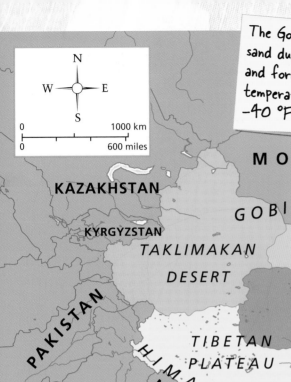

The Gobi Desert is not just sand dunes. It also has grasslands and forests. In winter the temperatures there can fall to -40 °F (-40 °C).

MONGOLIA

KAZAKHSTAN

Harbin

GOBI DESERT

KYRGYZSTAN

NORTH KOREA

JAPAN

Beijing

SOUTH KOREA

Tianjin

YELLOW SEA

TAKLIMAKAN DESERT

Huang He River

PAKISTAN

Xi'an

Shanghai

EAST CHINA SEA

TIBETAN PLATEAU

Chang Jiang River

Chengdu

HIMALAYAS

Chongqing

NEPAL

GUIZHOU

TAIWAN

Mt Everest

BHUTAN

YUNNAN

Guangzhou

Mount Everest is the highest mountain in the world. It is 29,035 feet (8,850 meters) high.

BANGLADESH

Shenzhen

HONG KONG

MYANMAR (BURMA)

VIETNAM

LAOS

HAINAN

SOUTH CHINA SEA

PHILIPPINES

Shenzhen is the fastest-growing area in China. New factories are being built all the time. About 75 percent of the world's toys are made here.

Government in China

China is ruled by one political party. This is the Chinese **Communist** Party. The country is divided into thirty-three areas. Each one has its own local **government**. Twenty-two of the areas are known as **provinces**.

The yak is a type of long-haired ox. It lives in Tibet in western China. The yak has a thick coat. This helps it survive the cold Tibet temperatures.

government group of people that makes laws and manages the country

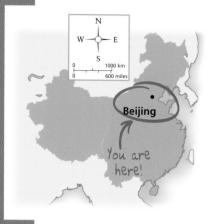

Exploring Beijing

The next morning you go to the center of Beijing. You walk across a wide open space. This is Tiananmen Square. It is a famous public meeting place.

Tiananmen Square is enormous. It can hold half a million people. Today it is full of young children and tourists. The children are flying kites. The tourists are making their way to the Forbidden City.

The Forbidden City

The Forbidden City is the largest palace in the world. It used to be the home of China's emperors (rulers). This building is over 600 years old.

The Forbidden City is one of the world's top tourist attractions.

➤

Desert winds

You look up at the sky. A yellow cloud is blocking the sun. High winds are blowing. These are blowing from the Taklimakan Desert (see map, page 7). They bring clouds of sand into the city. It's hard to breathe. Drivers can't see where they are going.

The **government** is building a wall of trees north of the city. It hope this will stop these **sandstorms** from reaching Beijing.

Olympics 2008

The Olympic Games are going to be held in Beijing in 2008. The city has improved its transportation for the Games. It made its airport bigger. Beijing has also developed a high-speed railway.

This picture shows Beijing's traffic during a sandstorm.

sandstorm strong wind that carries clouds of sand through the air

Climate and Landscape

China has many different types of scenery. There are also different types of **climate**. This is because the country is very large.

Cold north

In the north the summers are warm or hot. But the winters are bitterly cold. There is low rainfall. This causes serious water shortages.

Beijing winter

Beijing has hot summers. But the winters can be very cold. Winter brings freezing winds from the north.

The northern city of Harbin has extremely cold winters. Here people can build giant sculptures out of snow.

WORD BANK   climate pattern of weather in an area

Tropical south

The south has a **tropical** climate. Winters are warm. Summers are very hot and damp. During the summer, there may be violent storms. These are called typhoons. They bring extremely high winds. Typhoons can cause great destruction.

Skiing

Manchuria is a region to the north of Beijing. It is a mountainous area. The winters there are long and cold. China's largest ski resort is in Manchuria. It is in Yabuli.

China has some beautiful tropical beaches. This beach is in Shenzhen in the south.

tropical to do with the tropics, the warmest parts of the world

Mighty rivers

China's most important rivers are the Chang Jiang (Yangtze River) and the Huang He (Yellow River). Their waters help produce crops. The rivers are also used to carry goods across China.

Highlands

The Tibetan **Plateau** lies in southwest China (see map, page 7). This is high, flat land. The plateau covers more than one-third of China. It is difficult to live there. The **climate** is cold. The land is dry and rocky.

The Himalayas lie along the plateau's southern edge. This is the world's highest mountain system.

Lowlands

To the east lie the floodplains. These are low areas. They flood when the river water rises. The floodplains are China's main farming areas. Most people live here.

The Tibetan Plateau has some strange rock formations. They are known as "clay forests."

WORD BANK   dam barrier across a waterway. It controls the flow of water.

The Three Gorges Dam

A huge **dam** is being built on the Chang Jiang River (see map on the right). This is a massive wall across the river. It will help stop terrible flooding in the area. It will be named the Three Gorges Dam.

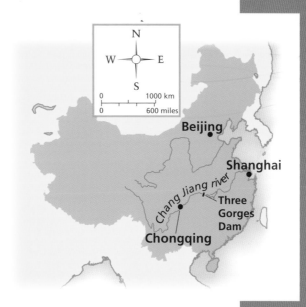

But the dam will drown hundreds of towns and villages. About 1.3 million people will have to move from their homes. Many people are worried that the project will damage the **environment**.

The dam project

The Three Gorges Dam should be completed in 2009. It will be 606 feet (185 meters) high and 6,500 feet (1,981 meters) wide.

When it is completed, the Three Gorges Dam will be the largest dam in the world.

environment the natural world or the conditions that surround us

A Bit of History

An inventive nation

Many inventions have come from China. They include paper, printing, and fireworks.

You decide to visit the Forbidden City. This palace is now one of Beijing's many museums. It shows visitors what China was like in the past.

Chinese dynasties

For thousands of years, China was ruled by different families. These families were known as **dynasties**. Each one is remembered for something special.

For example, the Xia dynasty ruled about 4,000 years ago. Writing was invented during their rule.

The Great Wall of China is 3,946 miles (6,350 kilometers) long. It stretches across northern China.

The Qin dynasty ruled about 2,200 years ago. The first Qin ruler called himself the First Emperor of China. He began work on the Great Wall of China. This wall was meant to keep out attackers from the north.

The Ming dynasty (1368–1644) is famous for producing beautiful pots and vases (see picture on the right).

These camels are carrying goods along the Silk Road. They are traveling through the Taklimakan Desert (see map on page 7).

The Silk Road

The Silk Road was an ancient trade route. It linked China to the Middle East and Europe. Goods were traded (bought and sold) along the way. The Silk Road runs through deserts and mountains.

End of the emperors

By the early 1900s, many Chinese were tired of having emperors. The people had suffered great hardships. They felt that the rulers had done nothing to help them.

The last emperor gave up his power in 1911. Years of war followed.

The Communist republic

In 1949 the **Communists** took control of China. The Communists believed that all people should be treated equally. China became the People's **Republic** of China. A republic is where people elect representatives to rule the country.

Mao Zedong was China's new leader. The new republic had little to do with other countries.

Mao's Little Red Book

The "Little Red Book" was a collection of quotations from Mao Zedong. Millions of copies of the book were printed. At one time Chinese people had to carry it with them everywhere.

A picture of Mao Zedong appears in the "Little Red Book."

Communist belonging to a political system called Communism. Under Communism, all property and wealth is owned by the state.

China changes

Mao died in 1976. The new leaders decided that China needed to change. They thought China should do more business with the rest of the world. Many new factories were built.

China can now produce goods cheaper than other countries. This is because people work for low wages. The country makes a lot of money. But there are still millions of poor Chinese.

This poster from 1949 shows crowds in Tiananmen Square. They are celebrating the start of the People's Republic of China.

republic form of government where people elect leaders. These leaders govern the country.

Getting Around

You want to explore more of China. But how do you get around this huge country?

The quickest way to travel is by plane. But flying costs a lot of money. Most Chinese people travel by train or bus instead. These can get very crowded.

Underground trains

Five Chinese cities have their own underground rail system. These are Shanghai, Beijing, Hong Kong, Guangzhou, and Tianjin (see map, page 7).

Rail travel

The train from Beijing to Hong Kong takes 24 hours. You can sit all the way or sleep in a bunk bed.

China has a large railroad network. More lines are being built.

These buses are taking people to work in Hong Kong.

N
W E
S

0   1000 km
0   600 miles

Harbin
Shenyang
Alataw
Urumqi
Dalian
Beijing
Shijiazhuaug
Luoyang
Nanjing
Xi'an
Shanghai
Wuhun
Hangzhou
Chengdu
Chongqing
Guilin
Shenzhen
Kumning
Kowloon
Nanning
(HONG KONG)
Sanya

Bikes and cars

All over China you see people on bikes. This is an important way of traveling here. There are more than 300 million bikes in the country.

In the last few years, some Chinese people have become richer. Many have bought cars. New roads are being built in the large cities. These are needed because of the increasing number of cars.

Car boom

Over 2.2 million cars were sold in China in 2004. But only three in every 1,000 Chinese people own a car.

These cyclists are waiting for the traffic lights to change.

City Life

You want to visit Shanghai. This is China's largest city. You decide to take the train from Beijing. This journey will take twelve hours. So you book a bunk bed on the train.

Pudong

Your train arrives at Shanghai at 7 A.M. You take a ferry across the Huangpu River. It takes you to Pudong. This is the new part of Shanghai. Many banks and businesses have their headquarters in Pudong.

Pudong has a very modern skyline. The Oriental Pearl Tower is 1,536 feet (468 meters) high. It is at the center of this picture.

In Pudong you head for the Oriental Pearl Tower. The view from the top is amazing. You look down on a city of 13 million people.

You can hear the noise of building work below. Everywhere you look there are new hotels and offices being built. New roads are also being built. Shanghai is a good example of how China's cities are changing.

The magical Maglev

The Maglev (above) is Shanghai's new city train. It uses powerful magnets. These lift the train above a special track. The Maglev can go up to 265 miles (430 kilometers) per hour.

Early-morning exercise

You get up at 6 A.M. the next morning. You take the **metro** (underground train) to Jing An Park.

There are already people in the park. They are performing a series of slow body movements. This is **t'ai chi**. It is a traditional Chinese form of exercise.

Rush hour in Shanghai

By 7:30 A.M. everyone has finished exercising. The sidewalks are full of people. They are rushing to work or school. Buses are filling up. Some people are stopping taxis.

T'ai chi involves slow movement and concentration. It exercises the body and the mind.

WORD BANK   metro rail system in a city area

The world's Chinatowns

Many cities across the world have their own Chinatowns. These are places with Chinese shops and restaurants. Some also have Chinese movie theaters.

Shopping has become a popular pastime in China's big cities. This is a crowded street in Shanghai.

t'ai chi a system of exercises. It is designed for relaxation and meditation.

Leisure time

People in cities like to relax by shopping and eating out. Many of them go to nightclubs and discos.

Lots of people enjoy the Chinese opera. This is a traditional entertainment. It combines music and drama. It also has acrobatics, which are gymnastic movements. But young Chinese are more interested in pop music.

Shanghai has many modern indoor ➤ shopping malls.

Hutongs

Chinese cities are changing fast. Many old buildings are being torn down. They have to make way for new roads and buildings.

Beijing's *hutongs* are an old type of housing. These houses are close together. Everyone living there knows one another. Many *hutongs* are being destroyed. This means that a traditional way of life is also disappearing.

City facts
- More than 500 million Chinese people live in cities.
- There are nearly 700 cities in China.
- China's biggest cities are all in the east.

This gateway leads into an old *hutong* in Beijing. *Hutong* houses are built around a small **courtyard**.

courtyard open space surrounded by walls or other buildings

Now you have to decide which other cities to visit. You look through a guidebook.

Hong Kong

In the past the United Kingdom ruled Hong Kong (see map, page 7). But in 1997 the United Kingdom handed the city back to China. Hong Kong is one of the world's largest financial

This market in Hong Kong sells all types of fish.

Hong Kong is a busy and exciting city. It is a mix of traditional and modern ways of life.

centers. This is a center for businesses that deal with money, such as banks.

Harbin

Harbin is an industrial city in the north. Many of its buildings look Russian. These were built when Russia constructed a railroad through Harbin.

Xi'an

Xi'an was once the capital of China. It has a history of more than 3,000 years. There are many important historic sites there.

Chengdu

Chengdu is famous for its parks and flowers. It lies in the middle of some of China's best farmland.

You can look at the map on page 7 to see where these cities are.

You can look at the map on page 7 to see where these cities are.

Seaports

The Chinese coastline is very busy. China makes many goods for other countries. Most of these are transported by ship. The main **ports** are: Tianjin, Shanghai, Hong Kong, Shenzhen, and Guangzhou.

Chengdu has a population of 10 million. Many people believe it is the cleanest city in China.

port place where ships load and unload goods or passengers

Life in the Countryside

Paddy fields

Growing rice needs a lot of care and hard work. The fields are known as paddies. They are flooded with water. The rice needs this water to grow. The fields have to be weeded all the time.

It's time to move on. You jump on a bus and leave the city behind. You gaze out of the window at villages and fields. You see a man walking behind a plow. A buffalo is pulling it.

Farming

Farming is very important in China. It provides food for the country's huge population. People and animals do most of the farm work. But more and more farmers are using machines. This means they can produce more food.

This farmer is plowing a rice field.

Terraces

In hilly areas farmers use every bit of land that they can. They cut steps into the hills. These are called **terraces**. The terraces stop the soil from being washed away. Some of the terraced fields are more than 700 years old.

Key crops
Some of China's main crops are:

- rice
- wheat
- potatoes
- corn
- cotton
- tobacco
- sugarcane.

Growing rice needs lots of work. This woman is weeding rice on a terrace.

terrace step or ledge cut into a hillside

Village life

The bus stops outside a small village. You get off the bus. Then you walk along the main street.

You see lots of old people. But there aren't many young people here. Most of them have left the village. They have gone to find work elsewhere. Then they send money home to their families.

Chinese families

In China parents, children, and grandparents often live together. This is particularly true in the countryside.

Farming is the main work in China's villages. This farmer and his wife ➤ are taking their produce to market.

Courtyard homes

You decide to have a look around one of the houses. You walk into a **courtyard**. Some hens are pecking around the yard.

The yard is surrounded by houses. One of the houses faces south. This house gets the most sunshine. The head of the family lives here. His grown-up children live in the other houses.

These village children are playing at the entrance to a courtyard.

courtyard open space surrounded by walls or other buildings

Inside a courtyard home

This **courtyard** house is like most other houses in the village. It has electricity. There's a small black-and-white television. But there is no running water. The children fetch water from a nearby well.

Inside, you see a table covered with food. There are rice dishes and noodles. There are pork, chicken, and vegetable dishes. All these foods are produced in **rural** (countryside) areas. The family invites you to eat with them.

These three boys live in rural China. They are on their way to school.

▼

Village schools

Chinese children start school at the age of six. They have to go to school for nine years. Then they take an exam. Those who pass can go on to a senior high school.

Many children in these rural areas leave school early. Their families need them to help with the farming.

This is a rural school. A rural school will receive less money than a city school.

People and Culture

More than a billion people live in China. This is nearly a quarter of the world's population.

The people of China

There are 56 different **ethnic groups** in China. These groups have their own traditions and languages. But everyone in China learns **Mandarin**. This is China's official language.

The Han is the largest ethnic group. About 90 percent of China's population is Han. Most of them live in the east. The second-largest group is the Zhuang. There are 18 million Zhuang in China.

Some Chinese people are only allowed to have one child. This is to stop the population from getting too large.

WORD BANK ethnic group people with the same culture or nationality

Some of the larger ethnic groups live in the north and east. The Chinese **government** has given these people more powers. For example, Tibetans have their own **autonomous** region. This means they have been given the right to rule themselves in some ways.

Tibetans are one of China's main ethnic groups. These girls are wearing traditional Tibetan dress.

autonomous being separate or able to govern itself

Sport

China is a sport-loving country. You want to find out more about sports and Chinese life. So you head back to Beijing.

Soccer has become very popular in China. You go to a match with some Chinese friends. Spectators shout and wave their flags during the game.

Other popular sports include tennis, gymnastics, and table tennis.

The Chinese enjoy many different sports. This group of young men are playing basketball in a city park.

Food

There is a wide variety of food in China. Different regions have their own style of cooking.

Rice is the main food. But people in Beijing and the north eat more bread and noodles. Fish is another important Chinese food. There are over 150 types of fish here.

In the cities you can get all types of food. This could be anything from hamburgers and pizza to duck's foot.

China tea

There is a legend that tells how the Chinese discovered tea. It happened when some leaves blew into the emperor's cup of hot water. This was more than 4,000 years ago. Today China produces many types of tea.

Wontons are a type of dumpling (dough ball). Some are filled with meat. Others are filled with seafood or vegetables.

Religion in China

Religion was forbidden in **Communist** China for many years. The **government banned** it. But now people are allowed to follow their beliefs. During your visit, you have noticed lots of temples.

People in China follow different religions. These include Islam and Christianity. But the main beliefs are **Taoism**, **Buddhism**, and **Confucianism**. Many Chinese follow a mixture of all three.

▲ This man is visiting his ancestor's grave. He is lighting sweet-smelling sticks (incense) at the graveside.

Taoism and Buddhism

Taoism is an ancient Chinese religion. It teaches people how to live in balance with nature. Buddhism teaches people how to find perfect peace. Buddhists believe that we are reborn after death.

Confucianism

Confucianism is a set of rules for living. It is based on the teachings of Confucius. This wise man lived over 3,000 years ago. He taught that people should love and respect each other.

There are more than 13,000 Buddhist temples in China. This one is in Yunnan **Province** (see map, page 7).

Wildlife and Environment

Animals

China is home to thousands of different types of animal. These include snow leopards, tigers, and elephants.

You decide to visit Beijing's zoo. This is a great chance to see China's most famous animal—the giant panda. It eats only bamboo. But bamboo trees are being cut down in China. Today it is difficult for pandas to live in the wild.

Animals and plants

China has an amazing range of different animals and plants. But some of its animals may disappear completely. This is because the places they live in are being destroyed.

There are now only 1,600 pandas left in the wild. About 1,000 more are in zoos and protected areas.

WORD BANK   environment natural world or the conditions that surround us

Environmental problems

China's forests are being cut down. When this happens, it is easy for soil to get washed or blown away. Then the land cannot be farmed. It can even turn into desert.

China burns a lot of coal. This produces a smoky fog over its cities. The number of cars in China is rapidly rising. They are also causing **pollution**.

The **government** is now planting trees all over China. It is making new laws to try to control pollution.

China has some beautiful landscapes. But they could be ruined by pollution and other problems.

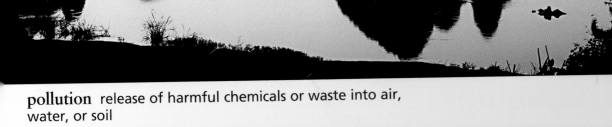

pollution release of harmful chemicals or waste into air, water, or soil

Stay or Go?

You've seen some of China's cities. You've seen how people live in the countryside. But there's still lots more to see. Do you fly home now? Or do you stay to explore some more? You have to decide.

Still to see and do

- The huge army of **terra cotta** warriors. These clay figures guard the tomb of China's first emperor. There are more than 10,000 figures and chariots.
- A three-day cruise down the Chang Jiang River.
- The caves at Longgong in Guizhou (see map, page 7). These extend through 20 mountains.
- The temples and stone forest of Yunnan **Province**. The stone forest is an area of amazing stone peaks (see picture on page 6).
- The Grand Canal. It was built 2,500 years ago. It links the Huang He and Chang Jiang Rivers.

Every year, thousands of tourists travel through Pudong Airport. This is Shanghai's main international airport.

➤

WORD BANK   terra cotta type of clay

The amazing terra cotta army guards the tomb of the Emperor Qin Shihuang. It is near Xi'an.

▼

A tourist hotspot

More and more tourists are visiting China. The World Tourism Organization believes it will soon be the world's top tourist destination.

Find Out More

World Wide Web

If you want to find out more about China, you can search the Internet. Try using key words such as these:

- China
- Beijing
- Chang Jiang River

You can also find your own key words by using words from this book. Try using a search directory such as www.google.com

Are there ways for a Destination Detective to find out more about China? Yes! Check out the books and movie listed below:

Further reading

Dramer, Kim. *People's Republic of China.* Danbury, Conn.: Children's Press, 2006.

Field, Catherine. *Nations of the World: China.* Chicago: Raintree, 2000.

Kalman, Bobbie. *China: The Land (Lands, Peoples, and Cultures).* New York: Crabtree Publishing Company, 2000.

March, Michael. *Country File: China.* North Mankato, Minn.: Smart Apple Media, 2003.

Morris, Noelle. *World Tour: China.* Chicago: Raintree, 2002.

O'Connor, Jane. *The Emperor's Silent Army: Terracotta Warriors of Ancient China.* New York: Viking Juvenile, 2002.

Movies

Crouching Tiger, Hidden Dragon (2000). This movie tells the story of a warrior's search for his stolen magical sword.

Timeline

1600–1027 B.C.
Shang **dynasty** rules China. During this period a writing system is invented.

1027–221 B.C.
Zhou dynasty rules. Iron is used to make tools for the first time in China.

221–207 B.C.
Qin dynasty rules China. Work begins on the Great Wall of China. Emperor Qin is buried with an army of **terra-cotta** warriors.

206 B.C.–A.D. 220
Han dynasty rules. The Silk Road is established. China begins trading with the West.

A.D. 960–1279
Song dynasty. Traders begin sailing to southeast Asia and India.

1280–1368
Yuan dynasty. Mongols from the north invade and take over China.

1368–1644
Ming dynasty rules. Work begins on the Forbidden Palace.

1644–1911
Qing dynasty rules. China's population begins to rise rapidly.

1839–1842
China is at war with Britain.

1911
The last Qing emperor gives up the throne.

1911–1949
Republic of China is set up. There is fighting within China. The Japanese take control of parts of the country.

1949
People's Republic of China is established. Mao Zedong becomes China's leader.

1966–1976
The Cultural **Revolution** takes place. During this time, schools are closed. Young people are encouraged to attack anything to do with old China.

1976
Mao Zedong dies.

1978
China begins a period of major change. The country opens up to foreign countries.

1989
Students protest in Tiananmen Square. They call for more freedom from strict laws. Troops kill hundreds of the protestors.

1997
Britain returns Hong Kong to China.

2001
China is chosen to host the 2008 Summer Olympic Games.

republic form of government where people elect leaders. These leaders govern the country.

China: Facts and Figures

The red in China's flag symbolizes the **revolution**. This was when the old **government** was replaced by the **Communist republic**. The large star represents the ruling Communist Party. The smaller stars represent the Chinese people.

People and places

- Population: 1.3 billion.
- Average life expectancy:
men—71
women—74.
- In China, a person's surname comes first. It is followed by their given name. So Mao Zedong is Mr. Mao not Mr. Zedong.

Technology boom

- There are 269 million cell phones in China.
- A Chinese person spends an average of 12.3 hours a week online.

China's industry

- Major industries: iron, steel, coal.
- The world's biggest shoe factory is in Guangdong **province** and employs 80,000 people.

WORD BANK   revolution replacing a government with a new one, usually by force

Glossary

ancestor person from who you are descended

autonomous being separate or able to govern itself

banned forbidden by law or by other rules

Buddhism religion that came to China 2,000 years ago. It teaches people how to achieve perfect peace.

climate pattern of weather in an area

Communist belonging to a political system called Communism. Under Communism, all property and wealth is owned by the state.

Confucianism a code of behavior. It is based on the teachings of a wise man named Confucius.

courtyard open space surrounded by walls or other buildings

dam barrier across a waterway. It controls the flow of water.

dynasty series of rulers from the same family

environment natural world or the conditions that surround us

ethnic group people with the same culture or nationality

government group of people that makes laws and manages the country

limestone rock created from the remains of sea animals

Mandarin official language of China

metro rail system in a city area

plateau area of high, flat land

pollution release of harmful chemicals or waste into air, water, or soil

port place where ships load and unload goods or passengers

province region that has its own local government

republic form of government where people elect leaders. These leaders govern the country.

revolution replacing a government with a new one, usually by force

rural to do with the countryside

sandstorm strong wind that carries clouds of sand through the air

t'ai chi a system of exercises. It is designed for relaxation and meditation.

Taoism ancient Chinese religion. It teaches people how to live in harmony with nature.

terrace step or ledge cut into a hillside

terra cotta type of clay

tropical to do with the tropics, the warmest parts of the world

Index